GREATEST OF ALL TIME PLAYERS

G.O.A.T. SOCCER GOALKEEPERS

Alexander Lowe

Lerner Publications ◆ Minneapolis

SPORTS THRILLS
MEET
RESEARCH SKILLS

Lerner SPORTS

Free Database Trial: **lernersports.com**

Lerner Publications Company
An imprint of Lerner Publishing Group, Inc.
241 First Avenue North
Minneapolis, MN 55401 USA

For reading levels and more information, look up this title at www.lernerbooks.com.

Main body text set in Aptifer Sans LT Pro.
Typeface provided by Linotype AG.

Library of Congress Cataloging-in-Publication Data
Names: Lowe, Alexander, author.
Title: G.O.A.T. soccer goalkeepers / Alexander Lowe.
Other titles: Greatest of All Time soccer goalkeepers
Description: Minneapolis : Lerner Publications, [2022] | Series: Greatest of All Time Players (Lerner Sports) | Includes bibliographical references and index. | Audience: Ages 7–11 years | Audience: Grades 4–6 | Summary: "Goalkeepers might be soccer's most important players. Learn about incredible goalkeepers and the saves, scoreless streaks, and championships that make them the greatest of all time"— Provided by publisher.
Identifiers: LCCN 2021016820 (print) | LCCN 2021016821 (ebook) | ISBN 9781728441139 (Library Binding) | ISBN 9781728448442 (Paperback) | ISBN 9781728444772 (eBook)
Subjects: LCSH: Soccer—Goalkeeping—Juvenile literature. | Soccer goalkeepers—Miscellanea—Juvenile literature. | Soccer—History—Miscellanea—Juvenile literature. | Soccer players—Rating of.
Classification: LCC GV943.9.G62 L68 2022 (print) | LCC GV943.9.G62 (ebook) | DDC 796.334092—dc23

LC record available at https://lccn.loc.gov/2021016820
LC ebook record available at https://lccn.loc.gov/2021016821

Manufactured in the United States of America
1-49884-49727-7/12/2021

TABLE OF CONTENTS

THE GREATEST GLOVES ON THE GLOBE

Soccer is the most popular sport in the world. In most places outside the US, soccer is known as football. Many countries have their own club leagues where pro teams play. Countries also have national teams for both men and women. National teams play other teams from around the world in international tournaments. All these teams make it very hard to tell which players are the best. But that is why it is so much fun for fans to debate the top players! Every fan has an opinion on who is the greatest of all time (G.O.A.T.).

FACTS AT A GLANCE

» IN THE 2015 WOMEN'S WORLD CUP HOPE SOLO DID NOT ALLOW A GOAL BETWEEN THE FIRST GAME OF THE TOURNAMENT AND THE FINAL.

» DINO ZOFF WAS THE OLDEST PLAYER TO WIN THE WORLD CUP.

» IKER CASILLAS (*PICTURED BELOW*) TOOK OUT AN INSURANCE POLICY ON HIS HANDS.

» LEV YASHIN IS THE ONLY GOALKEEPER IN HISTORY TO WIN THE EUROPEAN PLAYER OF THE YEAR AWARD.

Soccer has been around for a long time. Some types of the game are nearly 2,000 years old. The modern rules started in the 1800s. That was when many of the current goalkeeper rules began. By the 1900s, people all over the world loved the sport.

The goalkeeper is also called the keeper or the goalie. It is one of the most important positions on the field. The keeper is the only player allowed to use their hands. They wear a different colored jersey than the rest of the team. That is so the referees know who is allowed to catch the ball.

The goalkeeper can only touch the ball inside the penalty box. This is a rectangle-shaped box that goes around the goal. If the keeper touches the ball with their hands outside of that box, the other team gets the ball.

At the last possible second, Gianluigi Buffon of Juventus keeps a penalty shot from crossing the goal line.

German goalkeeper Nadine Angerer saves a shot in an international game against Nigeria.

The goalkeepers in this book are some of the greatest of all time. You and your friends may have other players you like better. Maybe some important athletes missed the cut. That's okay! That's what debating sports is all about.

GIANPIERO COMBI

Gianpiero Combi (*above right*) played his whole career for Italian soccer team Juventus. Juventus is part of Serie A, Italy's top club league. To this day, Juventus is one of the most popular club teams in the world. Combi was a big part of their success. He played for Juventus for 13 years. In that time, he helped his team win five Italian championships. Four of them were in a row.

Combi also earned 47 caps by playing for the Italian national team. His most important games were in the 1934 World Cup. Italy won the tournament that year, and Combi was the goalkeeper for the winning team. Many fans consider him to be one of the greatest Italian players of all time.

Combi did not allow a goal during the 1925–1926 season for 934 straight minutes. Few Italian goalkeepers have matched or passed this number. Many great keepers played during Combi's time, but none could compare with his greatness.

GIANPIERO COMBI STATS

International Wins		31
International Clean Sheets		13
Club Clean Sheets		145
Career Minutes Played		31,680

DINO ZOFF

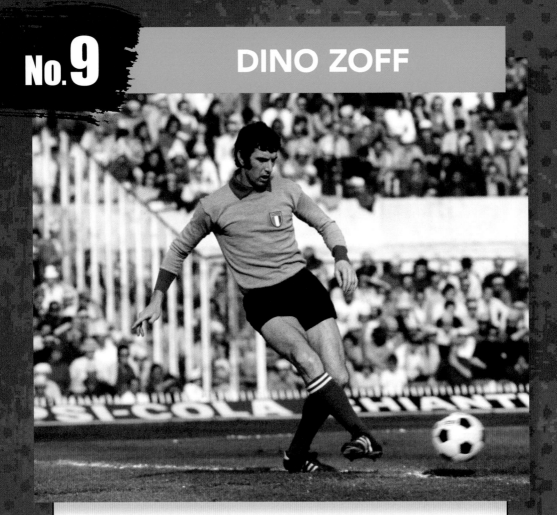

For several years, many considered Italy's Dino Zoff to be the greatest goalkeeper of all time. He was the first goalkeeper to captain a team that won the World Cup. On the club level, he played for Juventus. He won six league titles while at Juventus.

Zoff won the World Cup when he was 40 years old. That made him the oldest player to ever win the title. He also held the record for the most minutes in international play without allowing a goal. For 1,143 straight minutes from 1972 to 1974, he stopped every shot he faced.

In 2003, Italy named Zoff their greatest player of the past 50 years. Many great players have come out of Italy, so this was a huge honor. Zoff was known for playing smart soccer. He always made good decisions in the goal. After he retired from playing, Zoff became the Italian national team coach. He is well-known and loved in Italy. Fans all around the world respect Zoff as one of the greatest keepers to ever play the sport.

DINO ZOFF STATS

International Clean Sheets	62
Total Career Caps	112
 Clean Sheets Percentage	48.8
International Wins	62

Nadine Angerer is a true German legend. Her whole career was impressive. But nothing compared to her performance in the 2007 Women's World Cup. That year she set a record. She did not allow a goal for 540 straight minutes. In six full games against the best players in the world, Angerer stopped every ball that came her way.

The 2007 Women's World Cup was not her only great performance. In the 2013 European Championships, she allowed only one goal. She retired from the German national team in 2015 after earning 146 caps. With Angerer in goal, Germany won two Women's World Cups and five European titles. She also won seven league titles during her club career. In 2014, Angerer became the first goalkeeper to be named FIFA World Player of the Year.

NADINE ANGERER STATS

Total Career Caps		146
Age of International Debut		17
Women's World Cup Titles		2
Minutes without Allowing a Goal		540

HOPE SOLO

Hope Solo is the best US goalkeeper of all time. Her accomplishments are almost too many to name. She was a driving force that helped the US Women's National Team become one of the greatest in the world.

Solo and the US team won gold medals at the 2008 and 2012 Olympic Games. In the 2012 Olympics, only one out of 13 shots made it past Solo. She also won the Golden Glove Award in the 2011 Women's World Cup. This award is presented to the best goalkeeper at the tournament.

In 2015, Solo had an even better Women's World Cup performance. She shut out her opponents for nearly 540 minutes. She did not allow a goal between the first game of the tournament and the final. This performance earned her a second straight Golden Glove Award.

Solo was known for her fearless playing style. She was never afraid to charge at opposing players. She used her size and skill to knock the ball away. Solo had many excellent saves in which she lunged across the net and barely got a hand on the ball. The women's soccer world has never seen another keeper whose athletic ability has matched Solo's.

HOPE SOLO STATS

 Career Clean Sheets		102
Total Career Caps		202
International Wins		153
Age of International Debut		19

MANUEL NEUER

Even though Manuel Neuer was born in 1986 and is one of the youngest players on this list, he has already proven that he is one of the greatest of all time. One of the ways Neuer stands above his fellow players is his passing. Many goalkeepers are great at stopping the ball from going into the net. Neuer is also great at taking those saves and turning them into scoring chances for his team. He quickly gets the ball down the field to his teammates. Time and time again, he has helped his team score after he stopped a shot.

Neuer was recognized as the best keeper at the 2014 World Cup. He won that award again at the 2020 European Championship. In both of those tournaments, his forceful play sent many of the other teams' shots off target. In important games at the 2012 European Championship, Neuer had outstanding saves that quickly led to goals for his team. In 2020, he was named Best FIFA Men's Goalkeeper.

MANUEL NEUER STATS

	International Wins	57
	International Clean Sheets	43
	Total Career Caps	98
	Clean Sheet Percentage	46.2

PETER SCHMEICHEL

England's pro club league, the Premier League, is one of the most popular soccer leagues in the world. And Peter Schmeichel may be the best Premier League goalkeeper of all time. In the 1990s, Schmeichel helped lead Manchester United to great success in the Premier League. The team won five league titles. They also won the 1999 Champions League, which is a competition for all club teams in Europe.

Schmeichel was also impressive on the international level. He has the most caps of all time for Denmark's national team. He played 126 times for Denmark. His best international performance was in the 1992 European Championship. Schmeichel helped his team get an upset win against Germany, the top team in the world at that time.

Schmeichel's aggressiveness led him to score 11 goals throughout his career. Most keepers would be thrilled if they scored even one! When his team desperately needed to score, he would leave the goal and use his skills to help the offense. He was a powerful keeper and a true force in front of the net.

PETER SCHMEICHEL STATS

 International Wins   35

 International Clean Sheets   38

 Total Career Caps   126

 Clean Sheet Percentage   41

OLIVER KAHN

Oliver Kahn is known as King Kahn by his fans. He got this nickname for his aggressive style of play. Many other goalkeepers are content to sit back and wait for the shot. But Kahn is known for running at opposing players to take the ball away before they have a chance to shoot. This risky style of play has led to great success for Kahn. In his career in the German club leagues, Kahn won 21 trophies. Many of them were international championships. Eight were league championships.

Kahn also reached a World Cup final with the German national team in 2002. Germany lost, but Kahn won the Golden Ball award as the best player at the World Cup. Kahn is the only goalkeeper to ever win the award. No other German player has matched his dominance.

OLIVER KAHN STATS

International Wins	47
International Clean Sheets	29
Total Career Caps	86
Career Save Percentage	77

IKER CASILLAS

When it comes to Spanish soccer, few players are as famous as Iker Casillas. He played his first game for a pro club team when he was 16. He went on to lead his country to titles at the Euro Cup in 2008 and 2012. He also was in the net when Spain won its only World Cup championship in 2010.

Casillas was named the Best Goalkeeper in the World for five straight seasons. That is more than any other player in history. He is also the only keeper to captain a team that won the World Cup, the Champions League, and the European Championship. He won the Champions League three times. He also won the Spanish league five times.

Casillas was such a valuable keeper that he took out an insurance policy on his hands. His two-decade career is impressive. It is even more impressive how dominant he was for all those years.

IKER CASILLAS STATS

International Wins		69
International Clean Sheets		102
Total Career Caps		167
Club Saves		1,859

Gianluigi Buffon's outstanding career spans almost three decades. He made his first appearance for the under-16 Italian national team in 1993 at 15. He made his last appearance for Italy in 2018. He played at Italy's highest level for 21 straight years.

Buffon is known to have one of the best all-around games the world has ever seen. He has no weaknesses as a goalkeeper. He has a great knowledge of the game. Buffon also has incredible reflexes. His hands are some of the quickest and strongest in the world. This allows him to catch balls that other keepers might only be able to hit away. These qualities make him nearly impossible to beat.

Buffon holds the Serie A record for the most games in a row without allowing a goal. He did not miss a save for 974 minutes. That is more than nine games. He is the only keeper to ever be named Europe's Club Footballer of the Year.

GIANLUIGI BUFFON STATS

	International Wins	60
	International Clean Sheets	77
	Total Career Caps	176
	Club Clean Sheet Percentage	45.6

LEV YASHIN

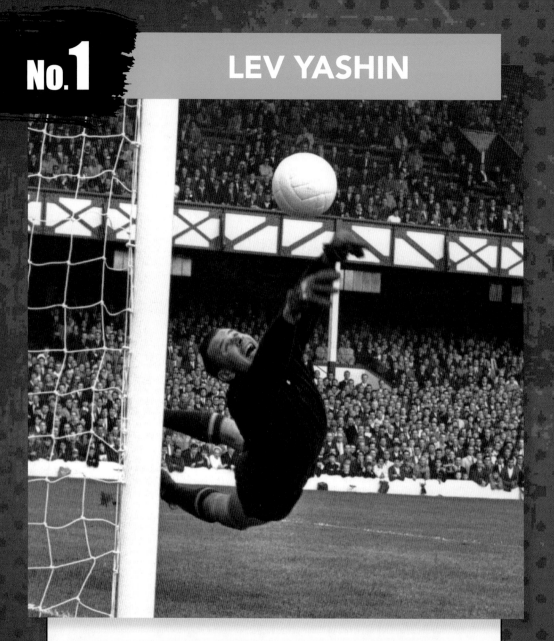

Lev Yashin was a true force as a keeper. He played 812 total games in his career. He had an estimated 480 clean sheets in those games. He is the only keeper in history to win the Ballon d'Or. The award recognizes the best overall player in the world. Yashin won the Ballon d'Or in 1963.

Yashin played his entire club career for Dynamo Moscow. In 20 years, he won five league titles. He was known to be fast and athletic. His quick reflexes helped him prevent many goals. He often used those reflexes to block penalty shots. Penalty shots are chances for an opposing player to take a shot on goal with no defenders. Penalty shots are taken close to the goal. These shots are very difficult for the keeper to stop. Yashin stopped 151 penalty shots in his career, more than any other goalkeeper in history.

Yashin helped Russia win the gold medal in the 1956 Olympics. Not only is he considered the greatest Russian goalie ever, but many also consider him the greatest goalkeeper of all time.

LEV YASHIN STATS

	Career Games Played	812
	Career Clean Sheets	480
	Penalty Shots Saved	151
	Total Career Caps	78

EVEN MORE G.O.A.T.

Many other great athletes have played goalkeeper. With so many amazing goalies in the world, even more could have made this list! Here are 10 others who almost made the G.O.A.T. list.

No. 11	BRIANA SCURRY
No. 12	GORDON BANKS
No. 13	PETER SHILTON
No. 14	ANDONI ZUBIZARRETA
No. 15	NEVILLE SOUTHALL
No. 16	SEPP MAIER
No. 17	SARAH BOUHADDI
No. 18	PETR CECH
No. 19	SARI VAN VEENENDAAL
No. 20	ALMUTH SCHULT

YOUR
G.O.A.T.

It's your turn to make a G.O.A.T. list about soccer goalkeepers. Start by doing research. Consider the rankings in this book. Then check out the Learn More section on page 31. Explore the books and websites to learn about soccer players of the past and present.

You can search online for more information about great players too. Check with a librarian, who may have other resources for you. You might even try reaching out to soccer teams or players to see what they think.

Once you're ready, make your list of the greatest players of all time. Then ask people you know to make G.O.A.T. lists and compare them. Do you have players no one else listed? Are you missing anybody your friends think is important? Talk it over, and try to convince them that your list is the G.O.A.T.!

GLOSSARY

Ballon d'Or: an award presented by *France Football* magazine for the best male soccer player in the world

cap: an international game played

captain: the official leader of a team

clean sheet: a game where a goalkeeper does not allow a goal

FIFA: a group that oversees soccer around the world

final: the championship match of a tournament

league title: a championship in a country's club league

offense: the players on a team who are trying to score goals

reflex: an action or movement that is made automatically without thinking

upset: when a game is won by a team that is expected to lose

LEARN MORE

The Best FIFA Women's Goalkeeper
https://www.fifa.com/the-best-fifa-football-awards/best-fifa
-womens-goalkeeper/

Buckley, James. *Soccer Atlas: A Journey across the World and onto the Pitch.* Plano, TX: QEB Publishing, 2021.

Doeden, Matt. *G.O.A.T. Soccer Teams.* Minneapolis: Lerner Publications, 2021.

Peterson, Megan Cooley. *Stars of Women's Soccer.* Mankato, MN: Black Rabbit Books, 2018.

Sports: Soccer Goalkeeper
https://www.ducksters.com/sports/soccer/goalkeeper.php

The World's Best Goalkeepers
https://everybodysoccer.com/even-the-goalkeepers-like
-to/2020/2/18/the-worlds-best-goalkeepers-2020

INDEX

PHOTO ACKNOWLEDGMENTS

Image credits: Christof Koepsel/Staff/pngimg.com, p.3; Todd Warsha /Stringer/ Getty Images, p.4; Paolo Bruno/Stringer/Getty Images, p.5; Zhizhao Wu/Stringer/ Getty Images, p.6; Christof Koepsel/Staff/Getty Images, p.7; Historic Collection / Alamy, p.8; The Picture Art Collection /Alamy, p.9; Staff/Getty Images, p.10; The History Collection/Alamy, p.11; Morne de Klerk/Stringer/Getty Images, p.12; Bradley Kanaris/Stringer/Getty Images, p.13; Rich Lam/Stringer/Getty Images, p.14; Mike Ehrmann/Staff/Getty Images, p.15; Alexander Hassenstein/Staff/ Getty Images, p.16; Martin Rose/Staff/Getty Images, p.17; Laurence Griffiths/ Staff/Getty Images, p.18; Stringer/Getty Images, p.19; Stuart Franklin/Staff/Getty Images, p.20; Laurence Griffiths/Staff/Getty Images, p.21; Gallo Images/Stringer/ Getty Images, 22; Denis Doyle/Stringer/Getty Images, p.23; Alessandro Sabattini/ Stringer/Getty Images, p.24; Pier Marco Tacca/Stringer/Getty Images, p.25; Central Press/Stringer/Getty Images, p.26; Central Press/Stringer/Getty Images, p.27; Nadezhda Shpiiakina/Shutterstock, Background

Cover: Christof Koepsel/Staff/Getty Images; Maja Hitij/Staff/Getty Images; Francesco Pecoraro/Stringer/Getty Images; Nadezhda Shpiiakina/Shutterstock